D0559953

THE MOON JOURNAL

A journey of self-reflection through the astrological year

BY SANDY SITRON

CHRONICLE BOOKS
SAN FRANCISCO

CONTENTS

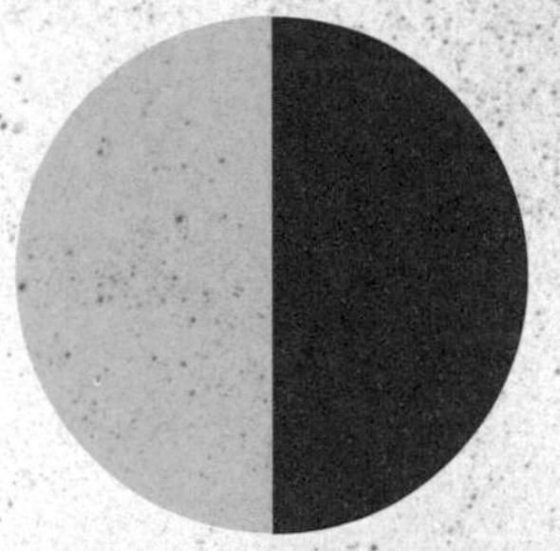

WELCOME TO YOUR MOON JOURNAL! 6

THE SUN AND THE MOON 11
Understanding the Moon Cycle 14

UNDERSTANDING THE MOON PHASES 17
Letting the Zodiac Guide Your Journey 20
Tips for Your Journal 22
Creating Affirmations 23
A Circular Dance 24
The Moon Sign 25

ROUTINES AND RITUALS 27
Morning and Evening Routines 28
Weekly Planner 32
The Full Moons 36

THE MOONS 39

Aries 41
Taurus 53
Gemini 65
Cancer 77
Leo 89
Virgo 101
Libra 113
Scorpio 125
Sagittarius 137
Capricorn 149
Aquarius 161
Pisces 173

Birthday Vision Board 184
Counting on the Moon 186
Herbs 188
Crystals 189

Pause and Reflect 190
About the Author 191

WELCOME TO YOUR MOON JOURNAL!

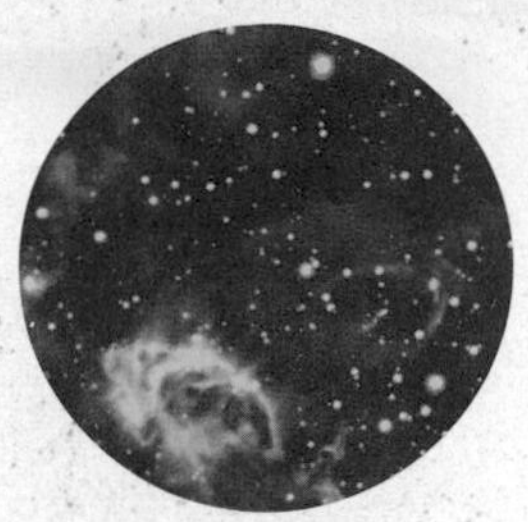

The moon is all about reflection. After all, the moon reflects the sun's light. Following the moon and learning how to harness its energy can help you reflect on your life, your dreams, your goals, and your relationships, and can be a great tool to help you live your best life. Self-reflection can inspire self-discovery. This journal will show you how.

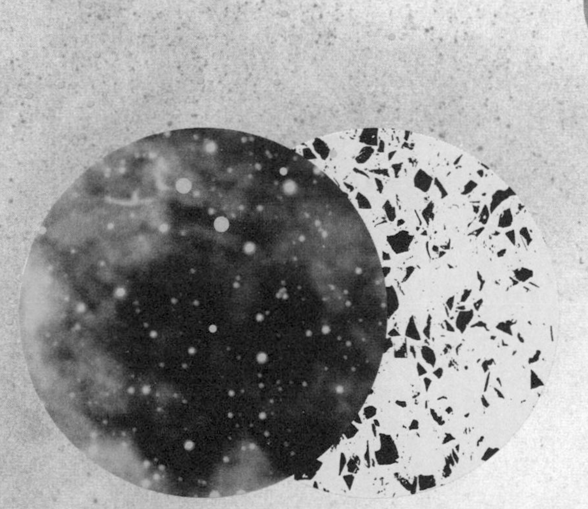

CONNECT WITH THE CYCLES OF NATURE

In our busy modern lives, it's easy to forget that we are part of nature. We know that vibrant green vistas soothe us. Vast wilderness inspires us. The limitless clusters of stars in the night sky fill us with aching wonder. And yet it's easy to feel detached from them all.

WE YEARN FOR CONNECTION

Understanding the moon's phases can help us reconnect with the cycles of nature. The moon's regular rhythm marks time for soulful self-reflection, boisterous jubilation, and everything in between. If we are in step with the cycles of the moon, the pace of life becomes easier and energy is restored. We may find that we feel more grounded and less stressed.

FOLLOW THE LUNAR TIDES INWARD

Living in harmony with the moon and stars connects us with our own internal universe. As we make our annual journey around the sun, every 30 days bring us a new life area to focus on. These life areas are defined by the 12 signs of the zodiac. Giving our attention to the themes presented by these signs helps us journey deeper into our understanding of ourselves.

Every 28 days, the moon moves through its own cycle, growing larger and smaller in the sky. As it grows (waxes) we develop. As it lessens (wanes) we release. The moon takes us on an emotional journey relating to the current zodiac sign of the sun. The sun lights up a theme and the moon helps us learn about that theme.

CREATE A VISION FOR THE FUTURE

Deeper self-awareness means knowing who we are and who we are becoming. Journaling and other daily practices can reveal our direction and purpose. A steady vision for the future allows us to move forward with confidence and ease. Each orbit of the moon can bring us closer to clarity.

WHO IS THE MOON? MAIDEN, MOTHER, CRONE

In ancient religions the moon represents the three archetypes of the feminine: maiden, mother, crone. Each phase represents a powerful feminine form. The feminine is the creative force. Follow the cycle to become a powerful creative force in your own life. When the moon begins her cycle as the new moon and develops through the waxing phase, she is the maiden with fresh new ideas. She can teach us about being new, unsure, delicate, innocent, excited, enthusiastic, vibrant, and changeable. When the moon becomes full, she is the nurturing mother. She brings ideas out into the world and can teach us about fostering life, nurturing, celebration, achievement, action, potency, and manifestation. When the moon wanes away, she is the crone, experienced and wise, teaching us about sagacity, contemplation, letting go, allowing, release, and liberation. She understands what needs to be released to make room for the next cycle.

The moon rules the feminine, the emotions, the right brain, images, symbols, the subconscious, dreams, intuition, psychic ability, and the water element.

WHAT'S IN THIS BOOK?

In this book you will find detailed descriptions of the moon, sun, and zodiac signs. You will learn about the moon's meaning and how to time your life according to the moon's cycle. Every month a new life area is described, with journal prompts and guidance as to how to use the moon to achieve certain goals.

At the start of each chapter you will find a blank monthly calendar. Add the dates and shade in the circles to represent the moon phases for each sign. This will help you keep track of and harmonize with each monthly moon cycle.

You'll find lots of space to journal, reflect, and process, as well as herbs, crystals, and rituals for each moon phase. There will be detailed suggestions for daily, weekly, monthly, and yearly routines to align with the cycles of the moon and sun through the signs. You'll learn about the mythology and symbolism of the moon as you follow the three moon goddesses—maiden, mother, crone—through the cycle. You'll create new intentions and develop them (new and waxing), find full expression (full), and finally let go to make room for the new (waning).

THE SUN
AND THE MOON

In astrology, the sun represents the essence of who you are and the moon represents your emotional nature. As the bright sun journeys through the zodiac over the course of a year, it illuminates different life areas—the zodiac signs. The sun shines a spotlight on the themes of your essential self-development. The moon moves through our sky much more rapidly, mimicking the rapid ebb and flow of the tidal waves of our emotions. Emotions are the language of manifestation. What you feel, you will manifest more of in your life. By changing your thoughts, you can change your emotions. Using a journal alongside the moon's cycle will help you choose the thoughts and feelings that you would like to have, so that you can manifest the life you desire.

THE SUN	THE MOON
Masculine	Feminine
Outward energy/Yang	Inward energy/Yin
Ego	Emotions
Essence	Reactions
Self	Creation
Identity	Fertility
Spirit	Intuition
Action	Receptivity
Linear/left brain	Cyclical/right brain
Fire	Water

The moon has a 28-day cycle.
There are two phases to this cycle: waxing and waning.

WAXING

- When the moon is increasing in size.
- Begins on the new moon and lasts until the third day of the full moon.
- Represents increase.

WANING

- When the moon is decreasing in size.
- Begins on the third day of the full moon and ends on the new moon.
- Represents decrease.

The two phases are divided into four quarters. These quarters are where we will focus our attention in this journal: new moon, first quarter, full moon, and third quarter. Each has a different energy and is best suited to unique activities, intentions, and rituals.

A WORD ON RITUALS

As you move through the moon cycle, you will be presented with rituals. A ritual is a symbolic activity. The language of the subconscious mind is symbolic. Acting out a ritual is a way to effect positive changes deep in your subconscious mind. There is no right or wrong way to create a ritual—use your creativity to expand on the rituals presented and make them perfect for you.

Understanding the Moon Cycle

Shown here are the eight significant parts of the moon cycle, along with their meanings.

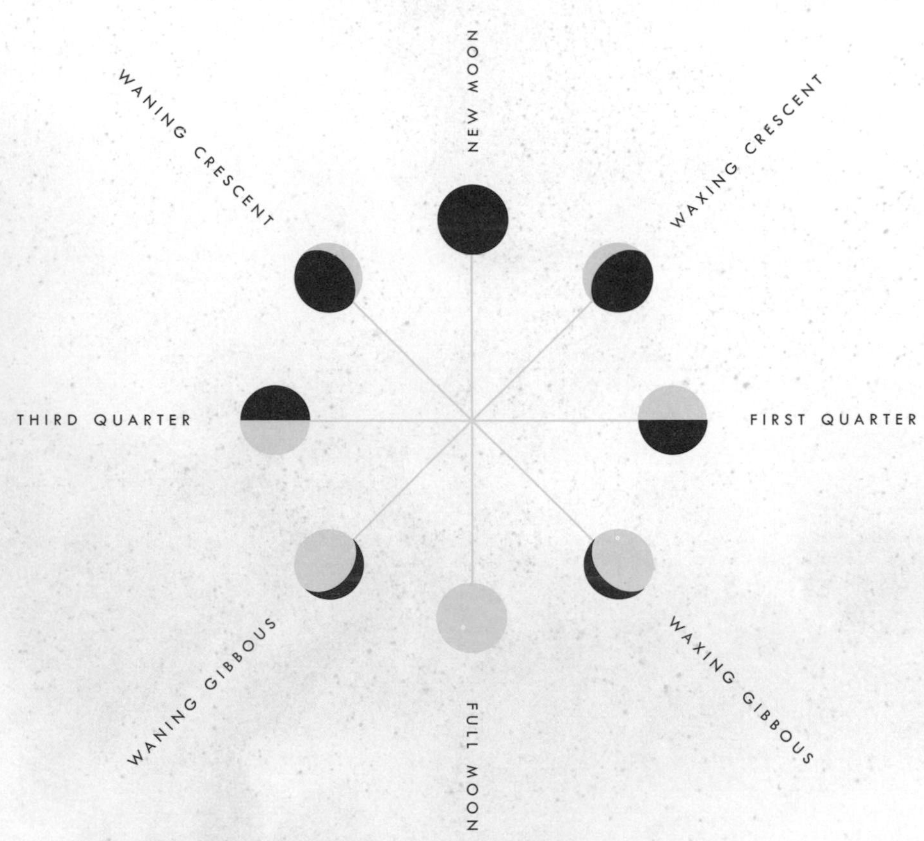

NEW MOON *set intentions*
Listen to your intuition and
allow new ideas to form.

WAXING CRESCENT *be curious*
Get excited about new possibilities.

FIRST QUARTER *develop*
Take action and
build momentum.

WAXING GIBBOUS *improve*
Refine and make improvements.

FULL MOON *full expression*
Celebrate your progress.

WANING GIBBOUS *share*
Reflect and teach others
what you've learned.

THIRD QUARTER *release*
Take stock of your life.
Find room to let go.

WANING CRESCENT *silence*
Rest and restore—get very quiet so
that you can hear your intuition.

UNDERSTANDING THE MOON PHASES

NEW MOON

The new moon is the perfect time to set intentions. At this time, it's not visible in the sky. It is sometimes called the dark moon or the hare moon.

The energy of the new moon is quiet. Without the benefit of the moon's light, our ancestors rested on new moon nights. Use this time to go inward and reflect on your desires. Set intentions for your life. Think of these intentions as seeds. What will you cultivate during the moon cycle?

ACTIVITIES

Quiet time. Alone time. Rest and recuperation. Pray. Meditate.

RITUALS

Every month, go through your previous new moon intentions and write the ones that you are still hoping to fulfill on a fresh sheet of paper, along with this month's new moon intentions.

Give your wishes to the moon. Write a letter to the moon telling her all about your hopes, dreams, goals, and intentions. Don't forget to say "Thank you!"

FIRST QUARTER MOON

This phase is all about development.

You planted your seeds on the new moon. Now it's time to help them grow! The first quarter moon can inspire you to take action, make decisions, and overcome challenges. Work towards your goals.

ACTIVITIES

This is a busy time! Do any work or activities that will support your intentions. Accumulate. Work. Socialize. Produce. Build momentum.

RITUALS

Say your intentions aloud while looking in the mirror. Imagine that you've achieved them. Create a feeling of gratitude as an energetic match for your intentions.

FULL MOON

When the moon is completely illuminated, it's time to reach full expression.

The full moon is the most powerful time of the entire moon cycle. Enjoy the full expression of life. Be fully engaged. Let the light of the moon energize you. This is your harvest. Harvest new internal realizations. Take note of your epiphanies. Harvest external success. Enjoy the life you are creating. Celebrate. This is a powerfully healing time. Send healing blessings to others.

ACTIVITIES

Play, sing, dance, draw. Harvest. Celebrate your accomplishments, big or small, with someone you trust. Share what you've discovered about yourself. Light a candle on your altar to honor your growth. Cleanse your crystals in the light of the moon.

RITUALS

Bathe in the moonlight. Allow the healing light of the moon to nurture and invigorate you.

Take a meditative and cleansing bath. Fill the bath with essential oils and cleansing Epsom salts. Meditate on your affirmations. Meditate on what you will let go of in the next phase.

THIRD QUARTER MOON

(also called the last quarter)

When the moon appears smaller and becomes half-illuminated, it's time to think about releasing.

The third quarter moon phase signals a time to let go. Release anything you no longer need to make room for the new! Meditate on what you've learned during the course of the moon cycle. Take stock of your life and notice if there are any relationships, commitments, physical objects, habits, or emotions you are ready to let go of. Letting go will free up energy that can be used during the next moon cycle. This is a quiet time to rest and restore.

ACTIVITIES

Cleaning. Using your journal. Meditating. Doing nothing. Resting.

RITUALS

On a piece of paper, write down what you are ready to release.

Burn the paper in a safe place. Say aloud what you are releasing as you watch the paper burn. When the paper has finished burning, breathe in a deep cleansing breath and smile.

Letting the Zodiac Guide Your Journey

As the sun moves through the zodiac during the year, it illuminates different life areas. Approximately every 30 days, the sun enters a new sign of the zodiac. As the sun "lights up" a sign, a theme is illuminated and the moon helps you to develop that theme. You will use this journal to contemplate each theme specific to each given sign and develop clarity and goals around it.

Find out what sign the sun is currently in and open the book to that section.

ARIES	21 March–19 April
TAURUS	20 April–20 May
GEMINI	21 May–20 June
CANCER	21 June–22 July
LEO	23 July–22 August
VIRGO	23 August–22 September
LIBRA	23 September–22 October
SCORPIO	23 October–21 November
SAGITTARIUS	22 November–21 December
CAPRICORN	22 December–19 January
AQUARIUS	20 January–18 February
PISCES	19 February–20 March

To understand the moon's journey through each theme, visit www.sandysitron.com/moon to find the upcoming dates of the new moon, first quarter moon, full moon, and third quarter moon in each sign, or keep a moon phase calendar on hand. Mark the days for the specific period on which you are working in the space provided in this journal. Use these dates as a framework to guide your journal entries through each theme and resulting moon phase.

This journal guides you through a cycle of self-understanding in the following areas.

Tips for Your Journal

Keeping a journal may increase mental and physical health and improve self-esteem. It's a great tool to help you grow. Use these tips to make your writing time extra-special.

GETTING STARTED

If you are having trouble getting started, just write stream of consciousness style, without thinking about it. Don't edit yourself or worry about grammar. Let yourself be free. Say anything.

MAKE TIME

Setting aside time for self-reflection is a powerful way to take care of yourself. Block out your own personal "moon time." Or decide to invite your friends over to join in! Bring out the telescope and call it a moon party (especially recommended during social butterfly Gemini, Libra, and Aquarius seasons).

CLEARING

Burn sage or palo santo to clear your mind and space before you begin writing. Say a prayer while you watch the smoke fill the room. "Only positive energy fills this space."

FOCUS

Light a candle to help you focus your mind before you begin writing. The candle flame can act as a reminder that you have dedicated this time for your journal.

Creating Affirmations

PREPARE FOR THE JOURNEY

An affirmation is an agreement you make with yourself. You are agreeing to create something new. Creating affirmations helps you grow in the direction that you desire, so that you can live the life of your dreams! There's an old saying that if you want something, you need to give your wish to the moon first. Here's how to make your affirmations/intentions moon-ready:

DEFINE YOUR DESIRE

Write what you want in your journal. Be specific: "Creativity and great ideas."

MAKE IT PERSONAL

Create an "I" statement that encapsulates your desire. "I want to be creative and have lots of great ideas."

NOW MAKE IT PRESENT TENSE

"I am creative and I have lots of great ideas." (This is a trick to convince your subconscious mind that what you want is happening NOW, not at some unknown date in the future.)

MAKE IT BELIEVABLE

Do you believe that your affirmation is possible? Or does it seem impossible? If it seems impossible, make the intention more believable. Add a stepping stone to your intention with words like, "I believe in the possibility that . . ." or "I choose to believe that . . ." or "I choose to . . ." Your affirmation becomes: "I choose to believe that I am creative and that I have lots of great ideas."

When you have spent some time with the affirmation, you may find it believable and you can then remove the stepping stone phrase.

ADD EMOTION

Decide what desired feeling goes along with your intention. Is it a feeling of peace? Excitement? Love? Joy? Make a note of the feeling. When you say your intention, try to create the feeling in your body. For example: "I choose to believe that I am creative and that I have lots of great ideas." (Desired feeling is excitement.)

CREATE AN ALTAR

An altar is a special space (a shelf, a corner, or even a whole room) that you can visit when you want to focus and meditate. It's a space that can help you connect with your higher self. You can put objects or images on your altar that remind you of who you are, who you are becoming, your goals, values, beliefs, and spirituality. It's a great place to keep reminders of your monthly intentions.

A Circular Dance

The sun and the moon each have unique cycles. The moon can be in any part of its cycle when the sun enters a new sign. So, sometimes the new moon phase will come first, but more often one of the other phases will precede it. We've arranged this journal with the new moon at the beginning of a section. But you can think of it as a continuous cycle.

WHEN THE NEW MOON COMES FIRST

Begin the phase by setting your intentions in alignment with the theme of the sun sign.

WHEN THE FIRST QUARTER MOON COMES FIRST

This is a powerful time to gain momentum. Create your intentions and begin to implement them.

WHEN THE FULL MOON COMES FIRST

Practice celebrating! Find something to celebrate in the theme of this sun sign. How did you feel about this last year? How do you feel now? Now develop new goals in relation to this sign's theme. You may also decide to review your intentions from the last new moon and celebrate how these have developed.

WHEN THE THIRD QUARTER MOON COMES FIRST

Think about the theme of the sun and decide what blocks need to be released in this area. Let go and prepare yourself for new growth.

By its very nature, a cycle is continuous. It's a circular dance. Move through the cycle with sensitivity and receptivity. If you find yourself becoming too logical, it's a chance to let go and lean into your intuition. The moon will support you.

The Moon Sign

The sun changes zodiac sign every 30 days, while the moon changes sign every 2.5 days. If you are tracking the moon with a moon calendar, you can also take note of the sign that the moon is in. This journal describes the energy of the signs. Use the energy of the moon sign to plan your day. For example, if the moon is in nurturing Cancer, take extra care of yourself that day. Maybe you would like to spend more time at home.

ARIES Take action, make decisions, start projects. Be a leader!

TAURUS Do things that feel really good! Take care of your money, body, and resources. Add beauty to your life.

GEMINI Learn something new. Think, write, and communicate. Socialize with friends and neighbours. Call a sibling.

CANCER Stay home. Take good care of yourself. Have family time. Reflect on your emotions. Cook.

LEO Be creative. Play and have fun. Find opportunities to be the center of attention. Dance, sing, draw.

VIRGO Organize! Take care of the details in your health, home, money, work. Be of service to others.

LIBRA Add balance to your environment—clean, organize, buy flowers. Add balance to your relationships—have an important conversation.

SCORPIO Reflect and forgive. Research. Tune in to your sexuality.

SAGITTARIUS Travel. Seek out inspiration. Be generous. Have fun.

CAPRICORN Work on a big project. Add systems to your life. Dedicate yourself to goals.

AQUARIUS Connect with a greater community. Create a vision for the future.

PISCES Meditate, dream, use your intuition. Be creative. Do nothing. Restore.

Now you are ready to begin! Follow the moon as she cycles through the year. Send your wishes to the moon and let her illuminate your path.

ROUTINES AND RITUALS

MORNING AND EVENING ROUTINES

Try out these routines when the sun is activating a sign.

ARIES

Morning routine *get moving*
Be active and productive in the morning. Get your body going with heart-pounding exercise. Then buckle down to work and cross one or two things off your to-do list.

Evening routine *cool it down*
While the sun is in the fiery sign of Aries, make your evening "cooldown" a conscious practice. Drink cooling peppermint tea. Listen to soothing music, stretch, and mindfully slow down your breathing.

TAURUS

Morning routine *luxuriate, then slowly get to work*
Have a slow start in the morning. If you like to exercise, give yourself plenty of time to warm up. After spending some time lounging, put in some time toward a big project. Slow and steady wins the race.

Evening routine *pamper yourself*
Taurus rules the physical body and the five senses. Attend to your physical body in the evening to help you relax before bed. Give yourself a massage, apply nice-smelling lotion or oils, listen to gentle music or the sounds of nature.

GEMINI

Morning routine *write, write, write*
The best thing to do in the morning during Gemini is to write. This could be in your journal, or you could try a more structured type of writing—an article, blog post, short story, or poetry.

Evening routine *set your schedule for tomorrow*
This is a time of busy mental activity. It's helpful for you to focus your thoughts and prepare for the next day by getting everything out of your mind and onto the calendar. Jot down some notes about your goals and plans for the next day so that you can rest easy.

CANCER

Morning routine *make a gratitude list*
Watery Cancer season can be emotional. You can start yourself off on the right track by creating a simple gratitude list. Evoking a feeling of gratitude can help you stay in a high emotional vibration throughout the day. First thing in the morning, write a simple list of five to ten things you are grateful for.

Evening routine *tea ceremony*
This is a great time to take good care of yourself. Nurture yourself with herbal tea or cucumber water.

LEO

Morning routine *make something*
Be creative. Make a painting, a song, or a salad. Use the morning to be carefree, joyful, and expressive.

Evening routine *read*
Slow down during fiery Leo season by appreciating the creativity of others. Read and gain inspiration.

VIRGO

Morning routine *self-improvement*
Take time in the morning to eat a healthy meal, drink water, and get exercise. Self-care will help you stay organized and focused throughout the day.

Evening routine *let go of your worries*
Close your eyes and imagine that each of your worries is a pebble in a small pile. Imagine each pebble and the worry it represents. Sweep it up into a dustpan. Empty the dustpan into a shoebox, cover the box with a lid and place it in a cupboard. Close the door and lock it if necessary. Your worries are now swept away. If there is anything that you want to think about later, it's still there for you. But for now, it's gone.

LIBRA

Morning routine *clean*
Libra is the only machine in the zodiac—the finely tuned scales. During Libra season, balance your environment by cleaning in the morning. Get rid of anything that you don't need.

Evening routine *enjoy dinner with a friend or partner*
Socialize and enjoy conversation in the evening over a beautiful and nutritionally balanced meal.

SCORPIO

Morning routine *meditate*
A morning meditation habit can help you learn to observe your thoughts and feelings during emotional Scorpio season.

Evening routine *reflect on your day*
Carve out time in the evening to write in your journal and come to new realizations.

SAGITTARIUS

Morning routine *read or write inspiring quotes*
Find inspiration to light your way forward.

Evening routine *listen to a guided meditation*
Allow yourself to take a mental journey as the sun moves through the sign of the explorer.

CAPRICORN

Morning routine *plan*
During practical Capricorn season, first determine your priorities for the day. Then take a quick glance at your plan for the day, week, and month.

Evening routine *set an alarm for bedtime*
To make the most of the next day, set an alarm so that you remember to go to sleep early.

AQUARIUS

Morning routine *make one business or network connection*
Aquarius season encourages community. Every morning, make an effort to create a new connection.

Evening routine *create or meditate on your vision board*
It's important to stay connected to vision during Aquarius season. As an evening ritual, work on a vision board. If you already have one, meditate on it.

PISCES

Morning routine *feel it out*
Follow your intuition in the morning. Ask your higher self about the best thing to do next. Intuition is strengthened through practice.

Evening routine *program your subconscious for dreams*
Before you fall asleep, ask to have a question answered in your dreams.

WEEKLY PLANNER

Did you know that a *planet* has ownership over each day of the week? Embedded in the root names of each day is the name of a planet. (In astrology, the sun and the moon are referred to as planets.) Use this guide to understand the energy of each day. It's an intuitive way to plan your week.

SUNDAY
SUN DAY

The sun represents the *essence* of who you are. It's your inner light. This is the day to connect with your image of yourself. Who are you becoming?

Do things today that are just for you. Focus on what would fulfill you the most and then follow the light of that idea. Today would be a fine day for some active exercise, connecting with others, a fun outing—or you could even do some work that fulfills you. Spend some time visualizing your ideal future. Meditate to connect with your true self. This is the *best* day to be creative.

Sunday/Sun Day Healing Activity
Start the day with meditation. If you are new to meditation, try seven minutes. Afterwards, write down three clear goals. Imagine yourself achieving these goals. Imagine feeling the satisfaction of having achieved these goals.

MONDAY
MOON DAY

The moon represents your emotions. It symbolizes your emotional needs and emotional reactions.

This is the best day to allow yourself to be in a receptive flow. Instead of focusing on action, focus on reflection. (An easy way to remember this is that the moon reflects the sun's light!)

Focus on nurturing yourself. Take some time to be alone if you're an introvert, or connect with a trusted friend if you're an extrovert. Meditate, reflect on the past, make space to feel your feelings, drift, and dream. Cook healthy, nourishing food, and practice Yin yoga.

Monday/Moon Day Healing Activity
Imagine yourself as a child. Let your mind go back to the age that feels most meaningful to you at this moment. Don't overthink it. Now, create a clear mental picture of yourself at that age. Where were you living? What did you look like? Who was in your life?

Welcome this younger version of yourself into the room. You can imagine that he or she is sitting with you. You can imagine a conversation. What would your inner child think of the space you are in now? Which object in the room might he or she be most interested in? Hang out.

You may decide to bring your inner child with you today. Maybe he or she goes to work with you. Imagine that your inner child is with you as you commute, eat, socialize, study, catch up on email, whatever. Maybe you bring them to a yoga class. Give your inner child a kind word here and there—make sure they feel safe and warm. You can even tell them, "You are safe. I am an adult now and I am taking care of you. You are worthy. You deserve love. You are enough just the way you are. You belong."

TUESDAY
MARS DAY

Named for the early Germanic god of war, Tiw. Mars represents your engine. It's what you have energy for, your ability to act, and your motivation.

This is a day of action. Where do you need to be active? And where can you be more mindful of your unconscious actions? This is a great day to start new projects. Be decisive and directed. You could choose to do some rigorous exercise today. Check in with your motivation. Where could you use a push? Be your own boss and give yourself some direction.

Tuesday/Mars Day Healing Activity
What are the things that you do without thinking? Checking email, having a cup of coffee, or eating when you aren't hungry are a few examples. Today we notice our unconscious actions so that we can heal. Here are your two exercises:

1) Do one thing at a time.
2) When you start to do anything, tell yourself what you are doing (either aloud or silently). For example, if you open your email, say, "I am opening my email."

These practices will help you slow down enough to notice the actions you are reaching for. If you notice you are automatically reaching for something, write it down.

Noticing a compulsive action is an amazing opportunity to have a revelation. Stop and ask yourself *why* you are reaching. For example, if you reach for a cookie, ask yourself, "Am I hungry?" If you aren't hungry, you are probably having an emotion that hasn't been processed. So, start to ask yourself what emotions you are having. Are you lonely? Sad? Frustrated? Angry? Disappointed? Is there another action that might help you work with the emotion directly? Crying is always a good one. Hitting a pillow might work. Calling a friend and talking about it could be great.

WEDNESDAY
MERCURY DAY

Mercury—or Woden, in Germanic mythology—represents your mindset: your thoughts, thought processes, and how you communicate.

This is an excellent day for writing projects. You can really focus on the details. And you can make some new connections. Learn about what's going on in your world. Pinpoint new areas of interest. Work on your language skills. Create more awareness of your thought patterns and beliefs. Basically, use your brain today!

Wednesday/Mercury Day Healing Activity
Start the day with seven minutes or more of meditation. Then, turn to your journal. You may use this time to reflect, or just to clear your mind.

Next look into a mirror, and say aloud, "I am willing to change." Look yourself in the eyes and repeat this statement ten times. This practice will open up your mind to new possibilities.

THURSDAY
JUPITER DAY

Jupiter—as personified by Thor—represents expansion, abundance, and gratitude. Jupiter is our jovial teacher, helping us grow through encouragement.

This is the day to connect with concepts of plenty, growth, and appreciation. Look for clues that you live in an abundant world. Circulate and meet new people. Consider your next expansion—what are your goals? Create a high feeling of gratitude within yourself—this vibration attracts luck. Today is a great day for uplifting exercise, having fun, and making a big impact at work. Think of this as your belly-flop day—take the leap, make a splash, and have fun.

Thursday/Jupiter Day Healing Activity
Start the day with seven minutes of meditation. Now write down five items on a gratitude list. This practice of gratitude reminds you of your abundance and supports your future expansion.

FRIDAY
VENUS DAY

Venus, as embodied by the Old Germanic god Frija, represents receptivity: harmony, relationships, and peace.

Venus = love.

This is the day to receive. Notice beauty and harmony. Take it slow. Do gentle exercise that makes your body feel really good. Remind yourself how good it is to be alive! Take time to nurture your relationships. Check in with a partner or a friend. Create harmony in your environment. But, most of all, open up to support. Put more emphasis on being rather than doing.

Friday/Venus Day Healing Activity
Start the day with ten minutes of meditation. Pray, and open yourself up to receive. Is there some support that you can ask for?

This is a day of receptivity, so give yourself lots of time to feel and be.

SATURDAY
SATURN DAY

Saturn represents structure and planning. Saturn is our authoritative teacher, helping us grow by showing us our lessons. Saturn is dedicated to integrity.

This is the day for organizing the foundations of your life. It's perfect for taking care of those things that require attention every so often, and set you up for success. It's a great day to work. Put in some elbow grease and get things done.

Saturday/Saturn Day Healing Activity
Start the day with ten minutes of meditation. Use today to plan your meals for the week, run errands, organize your calendar, organize your finances. Take care of your business. Take care of your body. As you do these tasks, remind yourself that you are deeply supported. Although this may seem merely practical, self-care is a building block of healing. Self-care leads to gratitude, which leads to trust in the universe.
Self-care = self-love.

THE FULL MOONS

The full moon has always been a special time for celebration and for marking the passage of time. Throughout history, cultures around the world have created unique names and meanings for each full moon.

JANUARY

Wolf Moon, Quiet Moon, Snow Moon,
Cold Moon, Guardian Moon
Stay home, reflect, begin a moon journal.

FEBRUARY

Storm Moon, Snow Moon,
Ice Moon, Hunger Moon, Horning Moon,
Quickening Moon
Prepare for spring, organize, and clean.

MARCH

Chaste Moon, Worm Moon,
Nymph Moon, Crow Moon, Dwarf Moon
Prepare the earth for planting and prepare yourself for change.

APRIL

Seed Moon, Pink Moon, Growing Moon,
Planter's Moon, Baby Moon
Plant seeds and create goals.

MAY

Hare Moon, Flower Moon,
Merry Moon, Bright Moon
Celebrate life and new growth.

JUNE

Dyad Moon, Strawberry Moon,
Rose Moon, Marriage Moon
Receive love and the first fruits of the season. Be joyful.

JULY

Mead Moon, Buck Moon,
Maiden Moon, Wort Moon, Thunder Moon
Enjoy, relax, receive.

AUGUST

Green Corn Moon, Sturgeon Moon,
Bay Moon, Ripening Moon
Collect and store.

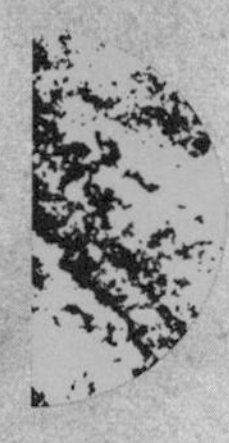

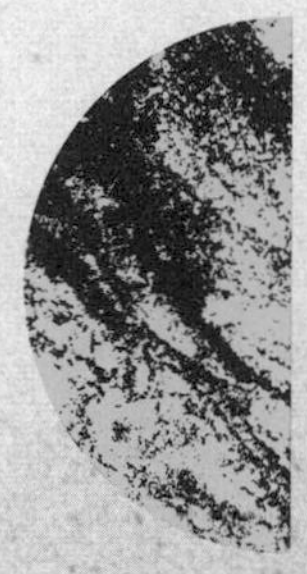

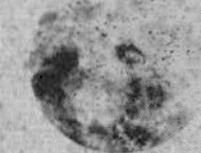

SEPTEMBER

Harvest Moon, Corn Moon, Barley Moon, Wine Moon, Autumn Moon
Harvest, celebrate, feast, share food.

OCTOBER

Blood Moon, Hunter's Moon, Shedding Moon, Hallow Moon
Honor ancestors, release.

NOVEMBER

Snow Moon, Beaver Moon, Winter Moon, Dead Moon, Frost Moon
Concentrate on inner growth and reflection.

DECEMBER

Oak Moon, Cold Moon, Yule Moon, Pepper Moon
Give gifts and make offerings.

A BLUE MOON

A rare occurrence! Once in a blue moon, there are two full moons in one month. The second full moon is called a blue moon.

ECLIPSES

A lunar eclipse can occur on a full moon. It supercharges the powerful energy of the full moon. A solar eclipse can occur on a new moon. This symbolizes a massive reset: a new beginning. Eclipse season occurs about every six months and lasts for about 34 days.

SUPERMOON

The moon's orbit is elliptical, not circular. Sometimes the moon is closer to earth and sometimes it is farther away. A supermoon happens when the new or full moon is at the closest point to the earth in its elliptical orbit.

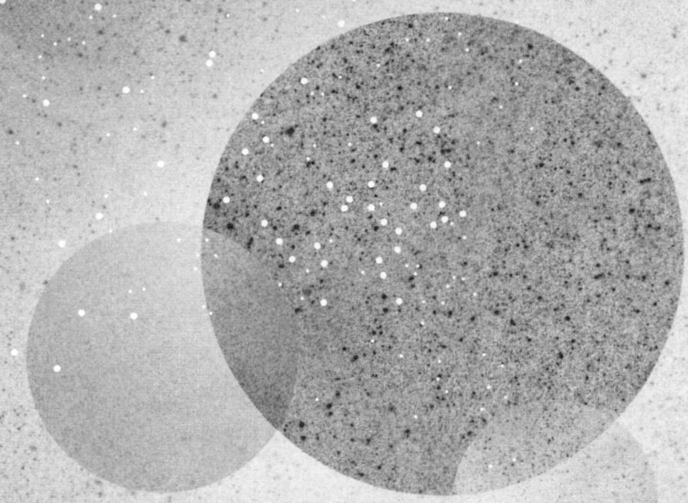

THE MOONS

ARIES

"I AM"

Confidence and Leadership

21 March–19 April

YYYY

S

M

T

W

T

F

S

NEW MOON: DD–DD

FULL MOON: DD–DD

WAXING MOON: DD–DD

WANING MOON: DD–DD

Aries season leads us into a new astrological year. Aries is like the newborn baby bellowing out her very first cry. It's a sacred announcement—"I am!" I am here. I am alive. I carry the spark of life within me. Aries energy helps you believe in yourself and take confident action as a leader. Throughout this Aries season, ask yourself: How can you show up with *confidence*? Where do you need to show *leadership*? When do you need to take *action*?

"I have faith in myself."

AFFIRMATION FOR THE MONTH

ARIES IS A FIRE SIGN

Fire is the "identity principle." Fire is the vital spark, the soul, the life-force; it embodies risk taking, leadership, passion, confidence, action, motivation, energy, and sparkle.

ARIES IS A CARDINAL SIGN

Cardinal energy is initiative energy. This energy helps you begin new projects and endeavours. Aries season is an excellent time to start a new job or hobby. You may choose to break a bad habit and begin a healthy one. It's time to hit the refresh button.

ARIES IS A PERSONAL SIGN

The first four signs are personal signs. These signs help us understand ourselves. How do you express yourself in a fiery way? Do you stand up for yourself? Do you take quick actions or make considered decisions? Do you have confidence? Do you trust yourself as a leader?

IF YOU ARE AN ARIES

This is your season for an upgrade. That's why birthdays are so important. Use the Birthday Vision Board in the back of the journal to help define your goals for the next year. As an Aries you are a natural leader, quick, decisive, active, charismatic, upbeat, and confident. Let the Aries season help you to expand these natural gifts.

NEW

The Aries new moon is the time to set new intentions about how to be confident and be a leader. Believe in yourself. Feel confident to speak out first in a meeting, begin an entrepreneurial endeavour, post on social media, or initiate a conversation. Maybe you are ready to bring something to the world as a leader—by developing a marketing strategy, getting onstage, running a half-marathon, or teaching what you know.

In which areas of your life could you stretch yourself to be more confident or more of a leader?

FIRST QUARTER

With the first quarter moon in the sign of nurturing Cancer, you may choose to be kind and gentle with yourself. As you develop your Aries qualities of confidence and leadership, a little kindness can go a long way! Treat yourself like a precious baby. Direct love and attention into the dark nooks and crannies of your psyche. Shine the moon's healing light into these places. Honor yourself and reflect back your own inherent worth. When you know your worth, it's easy to be confident! It's easy to take charge!

How can you put your intentions to have confidence and show leadership into action today?

FULL

The full moon in Libra marks the time when your confidence and leadership abilities come into full bloom. Take stock of your progress in this moon cycle or over the past year. If there is room for more growth, take action on it! Now is the time to flourish.

While Aries is all about your relationship with yourself, the opposite sign, Libra, is all about your relationships with others. The influx of affable Libra energy can help you be confident with yourself *and* use your confidence to connect with others. It can teach you to be a leader who is inspiring and works well with others.

Notice the small and big ways in which you've grown as a confident leader in this moon cycle or even over the past year. Record these in your journal. Don't be precious or critical in this process; instead be positive and encouraging. Celebrate your growth!

THIRD QUARTER

The third quarter moon in structured, earthy Capricorn can help you to be practical about letting go. Take this opportunity to release any emotion, belief, commitment, or relationship that is holding you back from full confidence and leadership. Letting go of what you don't need will free up energy to make space for new intentions. This is spring cleaning!

Take note of any blocks you may have around self-confidence and leadership. What are you ready to release?

TAURUS

"I BUILD"

Money and Self-Worth

20 April–20 May

YYYY

S

M

T

W

T

F

S

NEW MOON: DD–DD

FULL MOON: DD–DD

WAXING MOON: DD–DD

WANING MOON: DD–DD

Taurus season asks us to believe that life is a beautiful, abundant journey. Ruled by Venus, this sign controls the finer things in life. Taurus encourages you to remember that you are *worth it*. The symbol for Taurus is the bull—solid as a rock, stable, and secure. Throughout this Taurus season, ask yourself: Do you believe in *abundance* or do you fear scarcity? What would help you feel more *secure*? What project do you need to *see through* to the finish line?

"I have a strong sense of self-worth."

AFFIRMATION FOR THE MONTH

TAURUS IS AN EARTH SIGN

Earth is the "material principle." Earth is physical, sensual, practical, useful, abundant, receptive, verdant, grounded, stable, secure, helpful, organized, and structured.

TAURUS IS A FIXED SIGN

Fixed energy is lasting energy. This energy helps you stay directed and productive. Taurus season is an excellent time to focus your energy. You may choose to continue to work at something that requires patience and persistence. Keep going, you can do this!

TAURUS IS A PERSONAL SIGN

The first four signs are personal signs. These signs help us understand ourselves. How do you express yourself in an earthy way? Do you believe in yourself and your worth? Do you stay grounded? Do you feel connected to the abundance of nature? Do you trust yourself as a builder?

IF YOU ARE A TAURUS

This is your season for an upgrade. That's why birthdays are so important. Use the Birthday Vision Board in the back of the journal to help define your goals for the next year. As a Taurus you are grounded, nature-loving, dedicated, responsible, patient, sweet, and sensual. Let the Taurus season help you to expand these natural gifts.

NEW

The Taurus new moon is the time to set new goals about making money and building up your self-worth. These two seemingly separate things are actually linked, because strong self-esteem can help you believe that you deserve to make money and be comfortable. This new moon is the time to take an inventory of both your inner and your outer worth. Think of the Taurus bull as a stable, strong, enduring force of nature that is helping you build yourself up. Make plans to thrive financially and build up your self-worth. Maybe you could create a budget, savings plan, or investing goal. Remind yourself of the natural abundance of Mother Nature. Hold that metaphor close to your heart to remind yourself that you are naturally abundant and worthy.

What area of your life feels lacking in security? Write about how it would feel to be very secure in this area.

FIRST QUARTER

With the first quarter moon in the sign of Leo, you may feel more creative, outgoing, and ready to express yourself. A sunny, playful attitude can help you develop the Taurus theme of self-worth and abundance. Be yourself and express yourself. This active time is for creating inner security by expressing your uniqueness. You may decide to do some public speaking, dance, perform, make art of any kind, or spend time with children. Be playful. Build up inner security by having fun and being yourself.

Imagine how it would be to feel very secure in an important area of your life. Now imagine the next step you would take if you felt this kind of security. Write that step down and meditate on it every day until it feels possible.

FULL

With the full moon in Scorpio, celebrate the stability you are creating in your life. This may come in the form of self-worth or it may be the resources that you have. It may not be easy to see at first, but you'll find it if you look closely. Look for abundance everywhere and send out luminous moonbeams of gratitude. Taurus encourages you to build up self-assurance, while the opposite sign, Scorpio, represents letting go and merging with another person. The Scorpio full moon encourages you to be secure enough within yourself to let go of any need for control. It helps you learn that when you have inner stability, you can create healthier relationships.

Notice all the ways in which you've built up your inner or outer worth in this moon cycle or over the past year. Record these in your journal. Don't be precious or critical in this process—be positive and encouraging. Celebrate your growth!

THIRD QUARTER

The third quarter moon in Aquarius can help you to be innovative about letting go. Take this opportunity to release any emotion, belief, commitment, or relationship that is preventing you from thriving. A new way of thinking about things will liberate you.

Take note of any blocks you may have around money or self-worth. What are you ready to release?

GEMINI

"I LEARN"

Mindset and Community

21 May–20 June

YYYY

S

M

T

W

T

F

S

NEW MOON: DD–DD

FULL MOON: DD–DD

WAXING MOON: DD–DD

WANING MOON: DD–DD

Gemini season is all about building relationships. Ruled by messenger-planet Mercury, Gemini links ideas or people together. During Gemini season, consider how you form connections with others. Ask yourself: Where do you need to be more *curious*? Are you holding on to *outdated beliefs*? Do you feel connected to a *community*?

"I am open to growth and learning."

AFFIRMATION FOR THE MONTH

GEMINI IS AN AIR SIGN

Air is the "mental and social principle." Air is connection, thought process, sociability, communication, innovation, relationships, learning, writing, speaking, teaching, balance, breath, change, and aspirations for the future.

GEMINI IS A MUTABLE SIGN

Mutable energy is adaptive energy. It helps you refine, improve, and adjust. Gemini season is an excellent time to take stock of things and make necessary adjustments. Write down your thoughts and come up with ideas for improvements.

GEMINI IS A PERSONAL SIGN

The first four signs are personal signs. These signs help us understand ourselves. Reflect on your personal experience of the air element. How do you think about yourself? How do you speak to yourself? Do you believe in your ability to make friends? Do you feel curious? Are you able to think about your life with a sense of lightness?

IF YOU ARE A GEMINI

This is your season for an upgrade. That's why birthdays are so important. Use the Birthday Vision Board in the back of the journal to help define your goals for the next year. As a Gemini you are quick-witted, intelligent, social, friendly, and communicative. Let the Gemini season help you to expand these natural gifts.

NEW

The Gemini new moon is the time to set new aims for your beliefs and friendships. New ideas can inspire and invigorate you, so be open-minded and ready to learn. Get curious! In friendships, decide to give and receive support. Begin to feel connected to others in a new way. Learn about yourself through your friendships.

Brainstorm new ways to think about a problem you are having. Is there something new that you need from your friendships?

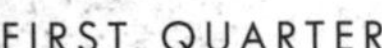

FIRST QUARTER

With the first quarter moon in the sign of practical Virgo, set routines that help you get in the habit of learning and building up your community. Envision action steps that will invigorate your mind—maybe you could sign up for a class or read something inspiring every day. You may decide to build in time to socialize, circulate, and network.

How can you act on intentions to learn and build your community today?

FULL

With the full moon in Sagittarius, you can celebrate your love, learning, and the sense of community and friendship you're creating. Notice how you've refined your beliefs or built your relationships in this moon cycle or over the past year. If there is room for more growth, take action on it! Evoke a sense of lightness during this process.

While Gemini is all about how you think and your local community, the opposite sign, Sagittarius, rules philosophy and travel. The influx of expansive Sagittarius energy can help you broaden your worldview. Learn about other people's beliefs to help you define your own.

Notice all the ways in which you've developed your mind and built your community in this moon cycle or over the past year. Record these in your journal. Celebrate clarity and connection!

THIRD QUARTER

The third quarter moon in emotional Pisces can help you to feel inspired to let go. Take this opportunity to release any emotion, belief, commitment, or relationship that is holding you back from a new way of thinking or connecting. Letting go of what you don't need will free up energy to make space for the next phase of development.

Take note of any outdated beliefs you may have in relation to learning and community. What are you ready to release?

CANCER

"I NURTURE"

Home and Family

21 June–22 July

YYYY

S

M

T

W

T

F

S

NEW MOON: DD–DD

FULL MOON: DD–DD

WAXING MOON: DD–DD

WANING MOON: DD–DD

Cancer season explores themes of nurturing, home, and family. Ruled by the ephemeral moon, this water sign helps you process and express your changing emotions. Cancer season is a time to develop feelings of comfort and love. Throughout this Cancer season, ask yourself: How do you *nurture* yourself? What can you do to make your home space more *comforting*? How would you like your relationships with your family members to *develop*?

"I nurture myself."

AFFIRMATION FOR THE MONTH

CANCER IS A WATER SIGN

Water is the "emotional principle." Water is emotions, dreams, the subconscious, images, symbols, intuition, psychic ability, spirituality, emotional security, family, home, ancestors, forgiveness, metamorphosis, and transcendence.

CANCER IS A CARDINAL SIGN

Cardinal energy is initiative energy. This energy helps you begin new endeavors. Cancer season is an excellent time to start new projects at home or new traditions with your family. You may choose a new routine or self-care ritual. It's time for fresh beginnings.

CANCER IS A PERSONAL SIGN

The first four signs are personal signs. These signs help us understand ourselves. How do you express your emotions? Do you allow them to flow? Do you trust your inner voice, or intuition? Do you take care of yourself? Do you feel comfortable at home?

IF YOU ARE A CANCER

This is your season for an upgrade. That's why birthdays are so important. Use the Birthday Vision Board in the back of the journal to help define your goals for the next year. As a Cancer you are nurturing, loving, romantic, warm, sincere, and gentle. Let the Cancer season help you to expand these natural gifts.

NEW

The Cancer new moon is a time to lay out your intentions for how you want to feel at home and with your family. Do you want to feel serene, creative, inspired, or playful at home? Do you want to feel safe and calm? What can you change to create that environment for yourself? How would you like your relationships with your family to feel? Authentic? Supportive? Loving?

How do you want your home space to feel? Describe your ideal relationships with family members. Write affirmations to give even more clarity to this vision.

FIRST QUARTER

With the first quarter moon in the sign of Libra, find ways to balance out the aesthetics of your home space. Create or develop goals for how you want your home space and your familial relationships to feel. Take action. Get rid of stuff you no longer need. Redecorate. Have a diplomatic conversation. Host a family dinner.

How can you take action to reach your goals for home and family today?

FULL

The full moon in Capricorn marks the time when your emotional security is expressed with a flourish! Review your progress in this moon cycle or over the past year. Is there room for more growth? Take action!

Cancer represents your emotional support, while the opposite sign of Capricorn indicates how you take practical action out into the world. This structured energy can help you implement any changes you are ready to make.

Notice the small and big ways in which home and family matters have improved in this moon cycle or over the past year. Record these in your journal. Look for any opportunities to express gratitude.

THIRD QUARTER

The third quarter moon in Aries can bring you a burst of energy. Use it to actively release. You need to have the freedom to feel your emotions and live authentically. Let go of any feeling, belief, commitment, or relationship that's blocking you from creating a safe space with your family and at home.

Write down your thoughts about your home and family. What emotion, limiting belief, pattern, commitment, or relationship are you ready to release?

LEO

"I CREATE"

Creativity and Fun

23 July–22 August

YYYY

S

M

T

W

T

F

S

NEW MOON: DD–DD

FULL MOON: DD–DD

WAXING MOON: DD–DD

WANING MOON: DD–DD

This sign inspires us to share our light with the world. Ruled by the shining sun, Leo teaches that creativity is how we express our individual nature. During Leo season, honor your creativity and be playful. Have fun! Throughout this Leo season, ask yourself: How do you express yourself *creatively*? Where do you need to be a little bit more *outgoing*? Do you allow yourself to be playful and *have fun*?

"I bravely express my creativity."

AFFIRMATION FOR THE MONTH

LEO IS A FIRE SIGN

Fire is the "identity principle." Fire is the vital spark, the soul, the lifeforce. It embodies risk-taking, leadership, passion, confidence, action, motivation, energy, and sparkle.

LEO IS A FIXED SIGN

Fixed energy is lasting energy. This energy helps you keep stay directed and productive. Leo season is an excellent time to focus your energy. You may choose to continue to work at something that requires passionate determination. Keep going, you can do this!

LEO IS AN INTERPERSONAL SIGN

The interpersonal signs help us share with another person. They help us learn about relationships. How do you share your creativity with others? Do you believe in your uniqueness enough to let other people see how special you are? Do you show honor and respect to others, even if you hold different perspectives?

IF YOU ARE A LEO

This is your season for an upgrade. That's why birthdays are so important. Use the Birthday Vision Board in the back of the journal to help define your goals for the next year. As a Leo you are big-hearted, generous, creative, playful, fun-loving, spirited, and noble. Let the Leo season help you to expand these natural gifts.

NEW

The Leo new moon is the time to set goals for sharing your creativity. Whether you consider yourself to be a creative person or not, we all show creativity in our own unique way. What is your stage and who is your audience? How would you like to feel when you express yourself? Can you get out of your own way and let the creative experience be playful and fun?

How do you want the experience of self-expression to feel?

FIRST QUARTER

With the first quarter moon in Scorpio, dig a little deeper emotionally as you create and develop your Leo intentions. What old conditioning or fear needs to be upgraded as you activate your creativity? Heal yourself by taking action. Express your uniqueness to the world.

Is there an old fear blocking your self-expression? What creative action are you ready to take?

FULL

The full moon in Aquarius allows you to bring your blossoming self-expression to full flower. Inspire feelings of joy within yourself. Evoke an experience of gratitude. Be childlike in your playfulness. Leo teaches us about our individuality, while the opposite sign, Aquarius, shows us how we can come together in community. Share your gifts with the world. Don't worry about being the best—just look for opportunities to participate.

Write about all the ways in which you've flourished creatively in this moon cycle, or over the past year.

THIRD QUARTER

The third quarter moon in earthy Taurus can help you to be straightforward about letting go. Notice any emotion, belief, commitment, or relationship that is holding you back from feeling generous with your creativity. Simply release.

Take note of any blocks you may have in relation to self-expression and playfulness. What are you ready to release?

VIRGO

"I IMPROVE"

Health and Habits

23 August–22 September

YYYY

S

M

T

W

T

F

S

NEW MOON: DD–DD

FULL MOON: DD–DD

WAXING MOON: DD–DD

WANING MOON: DD–DD

Virgo season presents an opportunity to improve your health and habits. Virgo makes the world a better place, one detail at a time. Use this energy to focus on refining your practices and general organization. This sign is dedicated to service: Virgo reminds us that to serve at the highest level, we need to take good care of ourselves. Throughout this Virgo season, ask yourself: What are your *self-care practices*? How do you feel called to *assist others*? What *habits and routines* in your life could be improved? How does *general organization* help you succeed?

"I am in tune with my body."

AFFIRMATION FOR THE MONTH

VIRGO IS AN EARTH SIGN

Earth is the "material principle." Earth is the body, the environment, sensuality, abundance, money, time, resources, connection with Mother Earth and nature, stability, security, service, organization, and structure.

VIRGO IS A MUTABLE SIGN

Mutable energy is adaptive energy. This energy helps you refine, improve, and adjust. Virgo season is an excellent time to take stock of things and make necessary adjustments. Write down your thoughts and come up with ideas for improvements.

VIRGO IS AN INTERPERSONAL SIGN

The interpersonal signs help us share with another person. They help us learn about relationships. Virgo works to improve life and share those earthy, grounded improvements with others through acts of service.

IF YOU ARE A VIRGO

This is your season for an upgrade. That's why birthdays are so important. Use the Birthday Vision Board in the back of the journal to help define your goals for the next year. As a Virgo you are refined, organized, disciplined, hard-working, kind, and modest. Let the Virgo season help you to expand these natural gifts.

NEW

The Virgo new moon is the time to lay down your intentions for self-care, organization, and service. Identify healthy new habits and improvements you'd like to implement. Focus on the details of your life—what you eat, your schedule, how your papers are organized, your exercise routine. Do some planning and decide on simple goals. At the new moon, create a vision for how you would like your average day to feel.

How do you want to feel in your body throughout the day? What changes would support this vision?

FIRST QUARTER

The first quarter moon is in the sign of Sagittarius. This ebullient archer encourages you to take aim and shoot for your goals. Step back and get a wide-angle view of what's important to you, then zero in on the details and make necessary adjustments. This is a time for definitive action.

How can you put your plans for health and new habits into action today?

FULL

The full moon in Pisces marks the time when the effects of your healthy habits and organization begin to show. Evaluate your progress in this moon cycle or over the past year. If there is room for more growth, make it happen!

Virgo rules the earthly plane, while the opposite sign of Pisces rules the spiritual plane. At the full moon, blend the energies of these two signs harmoniously. Explore meditation, prayer, and gratitude as practical and spiritual self-care techniques.

What are you grateful for?

THIRD QUARTER

The third quarter moon in inquisitive Gemini can make you more curious as to what you're ready to let go of. Take this opportunity to release any emotion, belief, commitment, or relationship that is holding you back from feeling really good on a daily basis.

In a very gentle and loving way, record the habits and routines that are no longer working for you. What are you ready to release?

LIBRA

"I BALANCE"

Relationships and Equality

23 September–22 October

YYYY

S

M

T

W

T

F

S

NEW MOON: DD–DD

FULL MOON: DD–DD

WAXING MOON: DD–DD

WANING MOON: DD–DD

Libra is the only sign symbolized by a machine—the scales. In Libra season, we learn how to find balance within ourselves, our environment, and our relationships. This intellectual air sign helps us grasp the concept of diplomacy, teaching us how to find compromise. Throughout this Libra season, ask yourself: Am I truly *listening*? Can I communicate without putting the other person *on the defensive*? What area of my life could benefit from more *balance*?

"I create balance in my life."

AFFIRMATION FOR THE MONTH

LIBRA IS AN AIR SIGN

Air is the "mental and social principle." Air is connection, thought process, sociability, communication, innovation, relationships, learning, writing, speaking, teaching, balance, breath, change, and aspirations for the future.

LIBRA IS A CARDINAL SIGN

Cardinal energy is initiative energy. This energy helps you begin new projects and endeavours. Libra season is an excellent time to create balance in your life or start a new partnership. Begin more moderate habits.

LIBRA IS AN INTERPERSONAL SIGN

The interpersonal signs help us share with another person. They help us learn about relationships. How do you share your thoughts with others? Do you make an effort to understand what it's like to walk in someone else's shoes, while also respecting your own experience?

IF YOU ARE A LIBRA

This is your season for an upgrade. That's why birthdays are so important. Use the Birthday Vision Board in the back of the journal to help define your goals for the next year. As a Libra you are diplomatic, charming, amiable, intelligent, fair, balanced, elegant, and polite. Let the Libra season help you to expand these natural gifts.

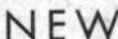

NEW

At the Libra new moon, set goals for how you want to communicate in your relationships and find balance in your life. Have you been thinking and speaking in a way that's too passive or too aggressive? If so, aim to learn to communicate more assertively. If you've been working too hard, aim to rest more. If you've been too scattered, aim for focus. It's all about finding balance.

In which areas of your life could you stretch yourself to find more balance?

FIRST QUARTER

With the first quarter moon in the sign of practical Capricorn, you may choose to get more structured. Look for systems that will help you create balance in your life. Take action and implement these systems. Set your goals and follow them through.

How can you act on your intention to find balance today?

FULL

The full moon in Aries marks the time when you attempt to create true balance. Take stock of your progress in this moon cycle or over the past year. If there is room for more growth, take action on it!

While Libra is all about your relationship with others, the opposite sign, Aries, is all about your relationship with yourself. Aries energy can help you be very decisive and clear about what you need. Libra energy can help you keep in mind other people's needs as well. With both energies highlighted at the full moon, true diplomacy can flourish.

Set healthy boundaries. What projects, relationships, appointments, or work do you want to say Yes to? What do you want to say No to? Use this decisive time to clarify what you have energy for, so that balance finds full expression in your life.

THIRD QUARTER

The third quarter moon in nurturing Cancer can help you to be gentle about letting go. Take this opportunity to release any emotion, belief, commitment, or relationship that is holding you back from feeling balanced. Letting go of what you don't need will free up energy for new intentions.

Take note of any choices, attitudes, or beliefs that are blocking you from living your most balanced life. What are you ready to release?

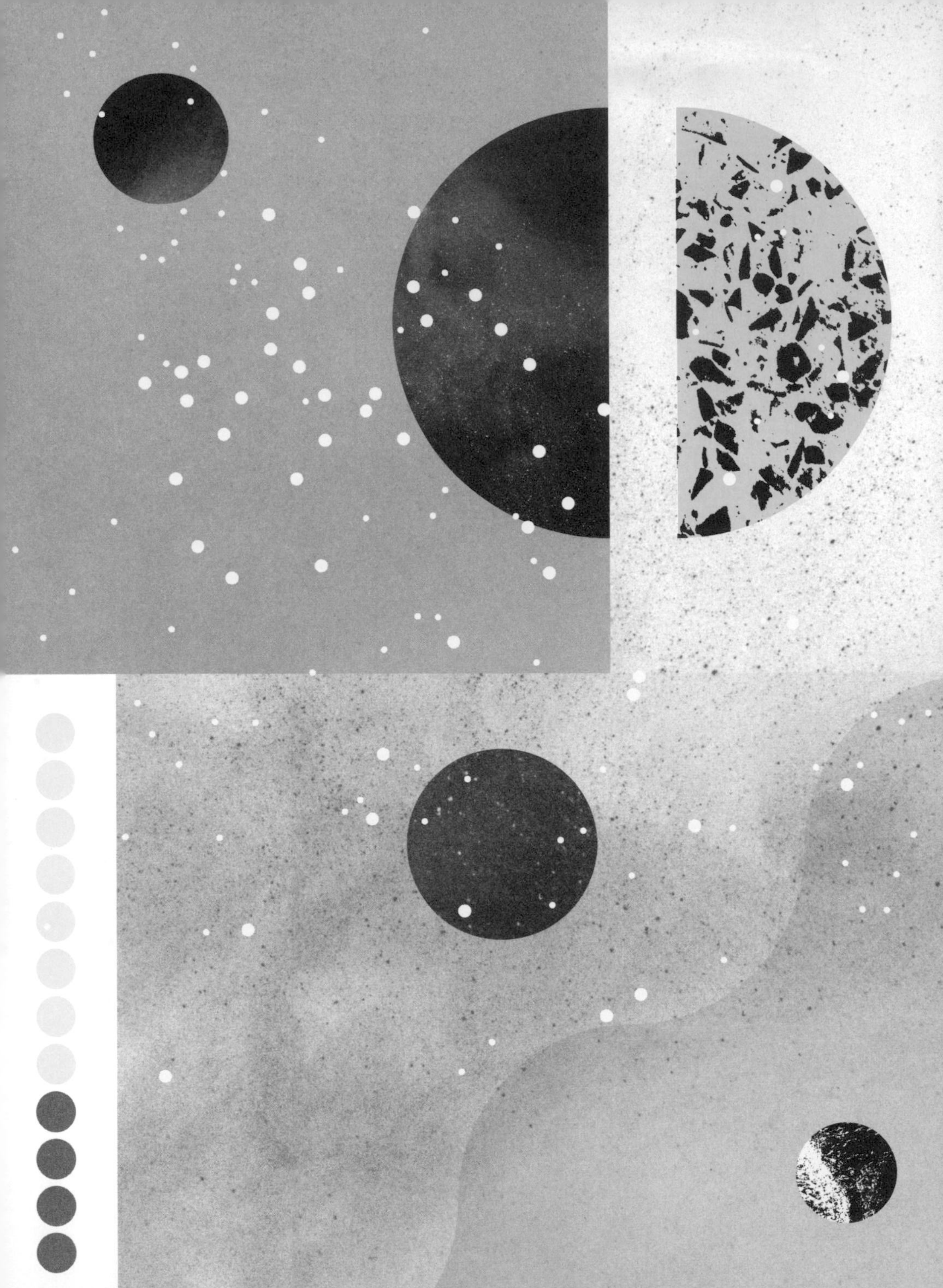

SCORPIO

"I EVOLVE"

Transformation and Forgiveness

23 October–21 November

YYYY

S

M

T

W

T

F

S

NEW MOON: DD–DD

FULL MOON: DD–DD

WAXING MOON: DD–DD

WANING MOON: DD–DD

Scorpio leads us through the cycle of life, teaching us how to transition. How do we let go, forgive, and move on? Scorpio also inspires us to merge in union with another person. This can happen physically, emotionally, mentally, and spiritually. Because this can make us feel vulnerable, the emotional water sign helps us understand themes of control and letting go. Throughout this Scorpio season, ask yourself: What are you trying to *control*? With whom can you safely feel *vulnerable*? Who are you ready to *forgive*?

"I am willing to change."

AFFIRMATION FOR THE MONTH

SCORPIO IS A WATER SIGN

Water is the "emotional principle." Water is emotions, dreams, the subconscious, images, symbols, intuition, psychic ability, spirituality, emotional security, family, home, ancestors, forgiveness, metamorphosis, and transcendence.

SCORPIO IS A FIXED SIGN

Fixed energy is lasting energy. This energy helps you stay directed and productive. Scorpio season is an excellent time to focus your energy. You may choose to continue something that requires patience and persistence. Keep going, you've got this!

SCORPIO IS AN INTERPERSONAL SIGN

The interpersonal signs help us share with another person. They help us learn about relationships. How do you share your emotions with others? Do you have intimate relationships? Do you practice forgiveness?

IF YOU ARE A SCORPIO

This is your season for an upgrade. That's why birthdays are so important. Use the Birthday Vision Board in the back of the journal to help define your goals for the next year. As a Scorpio you are emotional, tender, passionate, sexy, devoted, penetrating, and profound. Let the Scorpio season help you to expand these natural gifts.

NEW

The Scorpio new moon is the time to set goals in relation to transformation. It's time to determine how you need to release and move on. Have you been holding on to old feelings that need to be processed? Is it time to let go of an outdated belief system? Can you can interact with your sexuality in a new way? Maybe you need more intimacy in your relationships? Look for ways to let go and upgrade.

What areas of your life could benefit from a reset?

FIRST QUARTER

With the first quarter moon in the sign of Aquarius, you may find opportunities to think about transformation in a surprising new way. Reach outside your comfort zone and surprise yourself by doing things differently. React to an old situation in a new way.

How can you act on intentions for transformation today?

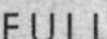

FULL

The full moon in Taurus marks the time when your personal transformation comes into full view. Take stock of your progress in this moon cycle or over the past year. If there is room for more emotional release, feel it fully. Express yourself!

Experience transformation and forgiveness in a way that can free up more energy for the new things you are ready to introduce into your life. Let the practical Taurus energy help you understand what is truly sustainable and what has got to change.

Notice the small and big ways in which you've shown forgiveness and transformed during this moon cycle or even over the past year.

THIRD QUARTER

The third quarter moon in Leo can help you to be joyous about letting go. As you continue to release any emotion, belief, pattern, or relationship that is taking up energy, do so with a sense of lightness. Be playful as you free up new creative energy.

Write down the patterns, emotions, or relationships you are ready to let go of. Read them or recite them to yourself while laughing or dancing. You could make up a silly song or drawing to describe the qualities you are ready to transform. Make it fun!

SAGITTARIUS

"I EXPLORE"

Wisdom and Travel

22 November–21 December

YYYY

S

M

T

W

T

F

S

NEW MOON: DD–DD

FULL MOON: DD–DD

WAXING MOON: DD–DD

WANING MOON: DD–DD

Sagittarius, the centaur, is half philosophical human, half instinctual horse. The philosopher is joined with the wild animal. The sign of the archer shoots the arrow and follows it, seeking higher levels of wisdom. Throughout this Sagittarius season, ask yourself: What do I believe is the nature of the *human experience*? How do people in different cultures *define their humanity*? Do I *feel truly free*?

"I seek new understanding."

AFFIRMATION FOR THE MONTH

SAGITTARIUS IS A FIRE SIGN

Fire is the "identity principle." Fire is the vital spark, the soul, the life force; it embodies risk-taking, leadership, passion, confidence, action, motivation, energy, and sparkle.

SAGITTARIUS IS A MUTABLE SIGN

Mutable energy is adaptive energy. This energy helps you refine, improve and adjust. Sagittarius season is an excellent time to explore options and make necessary changes. You may choose to brainstorm, research, and come up with ideas for improvements.

SAGITTARIUS IS A TRANSPERSONAL SIGN

The last four signs are transpersonal signs. These are the "big picture" signs. They help us understand ourselves in relation to the whole world. Sagittarius rules travel and philosophical exploration. What do you learn when you travel? How does exploration of the world, whether physical or philosophical, inspire you?

IF YOU ARE A SAGITTARIUS

This is your season for an upgrade. That's why birthdays are so important. Use the Birthday Vision Board in the back of the journal to help define your goals for the next year. As a Sagittarius you are wild, bouncy, cheery, ethical, scholarly, and unsinkable. Let the Sagittarius season help you to expand these natural gifts.

NEW

The Sagittarius new moon is the time to lay down your aims in relation to how you explore the world and find inspiration. Maybe you are ready to develop a philosophy, to explore the world through travel, to learn, or to teach. Collect inspiring quotes that you can refer to throughout this moon cycle or year. Set intentions to hone your personal philosophy.

If you had a personal mission statement, what would it be?

FIRST QUARTER

With the first quarter moon in the sign of Pisces, it's a good time to check in with your intuition to see which actions feel best. Find a quiet space and meditate. Then let your intuition guide you as to which actions will enable you to live your life according to your philosophy. Your inner guidance system can help you identify which ones will support your feeling of freedom.

What action can you take that will remind you that you are free? What action can you take today that will inspire you?

FULL

The full moon in thoughtful Gemini marks the time when your sense of freedom and wisdom finds full expression. Take stock of what you've learned and how you've developed in this moon cycle or over the past year. Maybe it's time to share your philosophy with friends or a larger community.

Have you been developing a philosophy in this moon cycle or over the past year? Express it in your journal and maybe even out in the world!

THIRD QUARTER

The third quarter moon in structured, earthy Virgo can help you to be practical about letting go. Take this opportunity to release any emotion, belief, commitment, or relationship that is holding you back from feeling confident in your unique wisdom and personal freedom. Letting go of what you don't need will free up energy and space for new intentions.

Is something blocking you from trusting your own wisdom? What are you ready to release?

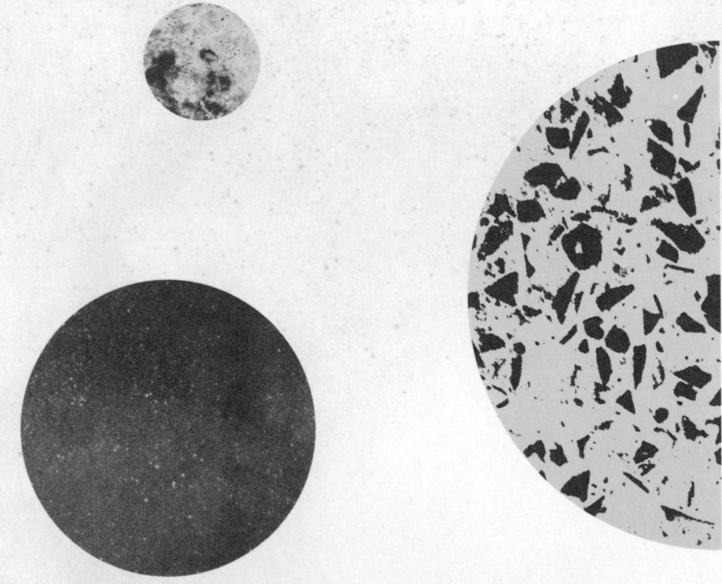

CAPRICORN

"I STRUCTURE"

Career and Goals

22 December–19 January

YYYY

S

M

T

W

T

F

S

NEW MOON: DD–DD

FULL MOON: DD–DD

WAXING MOON: DD–DD

WANING MOON: DD–DD

Capricorn energy helps us define career and personal goals. The goat wants to climb the mountain and reach the crisp, clear air at the top. For Capricorn, it all comes down to creating systems and structures that allow us to work at peak efficiency. Throughout this Capricorn season, ask yourself: What are your *career goals*? What are your *plans*? What systems do you need to *streamline* your work?

"I see myself as an authority."

AFFIRMATION FOR THE MONTH

CAPRICORN IS AN EARTH SIGN

Earth is the "material principle." Earth is the body, the environment, sensuality, abundance, money, time, resources, connection with Mother Earth and nature, stability, security, service, organization, and structure.

CAPRICORN IS A CARDINAL SIGN

Cardinal energy is initiative energy. This energy helps you begin new projects and endeavors. Capricorn season is an excellent time to start a new job or project. You may choose to start working towards a new and exciting goal.

CAPRICORN IS A TRANSPERSONAL SIGN

The last four signs are transpersonal signs. These are the "big picture" signs. They help us understand ourselves in relation to the whole world. How does the work you do contribute to the world? How does your work ethic compare to that of someone in another time or place? Do you trust yourself as an authority?

IF YOU ARE A CAPRICORN

This is your season for an upgrade. That's why birthdays are so important. Use the Birthday Vision Board in the back of the journal to help define your goals for the next year. As a Capricorn you are industrious, practical, structured, disciplined, prudent, and systematic. Let the Capricorn season help you to expand these natural gifts.

NEW

The Capricorn new moon is the time to lay out new intentions. Before you can set goals, it's important to know how you want to feel—and you must believe in yourself. As you craft your new moon intentions and goals, think about how you want to feel as you work, not just what you think you should do. For example, do you want to feel in alignment, filled with ease, productive, enthusiastic, or creative? Be specific.

How do you want to feel at work?
What are your work and life goals?

FIRST QUARTER

With the first quarter moon in the sign of Aries, you can take decisive action on your goals. Get ready to move forward and turn your intentions into reality. Don't overthink anything. Make your moves.

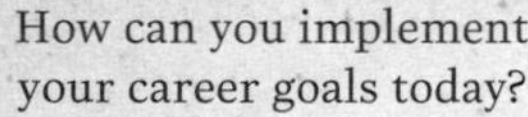

How can you implement
your career goals today?

FULL

The full moon in Cancer marks the time when your success comes into full bloom! Take stock of your progress in this moon cycle or over the past year. If there is room for more growth, take action on it. Now is the time to give birth to a new level of achievement.

While Capricorn represents the traditional archetype of the father, Cancer represents the archetype of the mother. At the full moon, be a good parent to yourself while giving yourself paternal support and maternal nurture. You can meet your goals and grow in just the right way.

THIRD QUARTER

The third quarter moon in Libra can help you to find balance by releasing anything that's taking energy away from your true goals. Take this opportunity to release any emotion, belief, commitment, or relationship that is holding you back from reaching the top. Make space for new directions.

Notice the small and big ways in which your career or life purpose has developed in this moon cycle or even over the past year. Record these in your journal. Don't be precious or critical—be positive and encouraging. Celebrate your growth!

Take note of any blocks you may have about meeting your goals in your career and in your personal life. What are you ready to release?

AQUARIUS

"I ENVISION"

Hope and Progress

20 January–18 February

YYYY

S

M

T

W

T

F

S

NEW MOON: DD–DD

FULL MOON: DD–DD

WAXING MOON: DD–DD

WANING MOON: DD–DD

Aquarius teaches us about clarifying our vision for the future. Ruled by the "Great Awakener" planet, Uranus, this sign is ready to shake things up. This is an innovative time. Throughout this Aquarius season, ask yourself: What is your *vision* for the future? How can you open your mind to *new possibilities*?

"I envision a better future."

AFFIRMATION FOR THE MONTH

AQUARIUS IS AN AIR SIGN

Air is the "mental and social principle." Air is connection, thought process, sociability, communication, innovation, relationships, learning, writing, speaking, teaching, balance, breath, change, and aspirations for the future.

AQUARIUS IS A FIXED SIGN

Fixed energy is lasting energy. This energy helps you stay directed and productive. Aquarius season is an excellent time to focus your energy. You may choose to continue to work at something that requires patience and persistence. Keep going, you can do it!

AQUARIUS IS A TRANSPERSONAL SIGN

The last four signs are transpersonal signs. These are the "big picture" signs. They help us understand ourselves in relation to the whole world. How do you convey your ideas to the world? Do you collaborate with others, near and far? Do you take yourself out of your comfort zone to learn from people who seem different from you?

IF YOU ARE AN AQUARIUS

This is your season for an upgrade. That's why birthdays are so important. Use the Birthday Vision Board in the back of the journal to help define your goals for the next year. As an Aquarius you are radical, cutting-edge, innovative, intelligent, progressive, and electrifying. Let the Aquarius season help you to expand these natural gifts.

NEW

The Aquarius new moon is the time to set new goals for your friendships, community, and future. How do you want to give to your community? How do you want to be supported by it? What is your ideal vision for the future of the world? What are your personal hopes, dreams, and aspirations?

How can you stretch yourself to be more positive and creative in your vision of the future? How does your positive view of the future directly affect your life?

FIRST QUARTER

With the first quarter moon in the sign of Taurus, choose to be persistent as you develop your Aquarius vision. Set your intentions and diligently meditate on them. Help your vision become a reality by keeping it at the forefront of your mind.

How can you take action to make your vision for the future a reality today?

FULL

With the full moon in Leo you get a boost of joyful energy. Remember that Aquarian vision you are creating? Bring it a little bit closer by making it feel playful and light. Be inventive as you create and express your vision of the world you'd like to live in. Make some kind of art or throw a party—have fun with it!

Brainstorm ways to use your creative energy to express your vision for the future. Singing? Dancing? Painting? Cooking? Gardening? Then take action!

THIRD QUARTER

The third quarter moon in Scorpio can help you to let go. Take this opportunity to release any emotion, belief, commitment, or relationship that is holding you back from your vision. Let go of the old so that there is room for the new.

Take note of anything that may be stopping you from truly believing in your vision for the future. What are you ready to release?

PISCES

"I TRANSCEND"

Intuition and Spirituality

19 February–20 March

YYYY

S

M

T

W

T

F

S

NEW MOON: DD–DD

FULL MOON: DD–DD

WAXING MOON: DD–DD

WANING MOON: DD–DD

Pisces season brings us to the end of the astrological year. Celestial Pisces holds the wisdom of all twelve signs and is ready to ascend to the next phase. This sign has full understanding of the earthly planes and can teach us about the other realms: the mystical, emotional, creative, and intuitive. Throughout this Pisces season, ask yourself: What do you *believe in*? Do you give your physical body time to *restore*? Do you feel connected to your *intuition*?

"I trust my intuition."

AFFIRMATION FOR THE MONTH

PISCES IS A WATER SIGN

Water is the "emotional principle." Water is emotions, dreams, the subconscious, images, symbols, intuition, psychic ability, spirituality, emotional security, family, home, ancestors, forgiveness, metamorphosis, and transcendence.

PISCES IS A MUTABLE SIGN

Mutable energy is adaptive energy. This energy helps you refine, improve, and adjust. Pisces season is an excellent time to meditate and connect with your inner guidance system to identify what is ready for adjustment.

PISCES IS A TRANSPERSONAL SIGN

The last four signs are transpersonal signs. These are the "big picture" signs. They help us understand ourselves in relation to the whole world. How can you feel compassion for people across the world? How can you feel connected to them?

IF YOU ARE A PISCES

This is your season for an upgrade. That's why birthdays are so important. Use the Birthday Vision Board in the back of the journal to help define your goals for the next year. As a Pisces you are ethereal, spiritual, mystical, magical, and intuitive. Let the Pisces season help you to expand these natural gifts.

NEW

The Pisces new moon is the time to set new goals regarding how to connect with your intuition and define your spirituality. Can you seek out new ways to deepen your dream state, intuition, and creativity? Can you trust that you are naturally intuitive?

What are your goals in relation to intuitive and spiritual development?

FIRST QUARTER

With the first quarter moon in the sign of Gemini, you may choose to be curious about how to develop your intuition and spirituality. Gather information and learn about different ways to expand in these realms.

How can you learn about your spirituality or discover tools to deepen your intuition today?

FULL

The full moon in Virgo marks the full expression of your intuitive and spiritual journey. Take stock of your progress in this moon cycle or over the past year. If there is room for more growth, take action on it! Now is the time to expand your mind.

While Pisces rules the spiritual, Virgo rules the practical. Make your spiritual growth highly practical through routines such as meditation and writing in your journal.

THIRD QUARTER

The third quarter moon in Sagittarius can help you to be philosophical about letting go. Release any emotion, belief, commitment, or relationship that is holding you back from connecting with yourself and your spirituality. Be inspired by your ability to release ideas that no longer serve you.

Explore your spiritual and intuitive development. What has felt different over the course of this moon cycle or over the past year? Take this opportunity to celebrate your growth.

Take note of any blocks you may have around your spirituality or intuition. What are you ready to release?

BIRTHDAY VISION BOARD

Happy birthday! The sun has returned to the sign it was in when you were born. Your star sign is illuminated by the sun's bright light. It's your personal New Year. A new beginning. Begin with vision. Begin with a wish. The ritual of making a wish when blowing out birthday candles originated as a devotion to the moon goddess Artemis.

To celebrate Artemis's birthday, ancient Greeks brought crescent-shaped cakes topped with burning candles to her temple. They shared their deepest wishes with her and presented the cake as an offering to ensure her good graces.

What wishes will you bring to the moon goddess?

The moon rules the right brain, the feminine, the intuitive, the visual, the symbolic, the subconscious. Images and symbols communicate your conscious desires to your subconscious mind, creating lasting, positive change.

WRITE DOWN YOUR WISHES FOR EACH OF THESE LIFE AREAS

Health
Relationships
Money
Career
Sexuality
Spirituality

Now find or make images that symbolize your wishes, and create a collage. This will be your Birthday Vision Board. Maybe you'd like to place it on your wall or altar. Refer to it at every new moon. Make adjustments as the year progresses.

COUNTING ON THE MOON

In the ancient world, the moon cycle was a way to mark the passage of time. It was especially helpful in calculating the optimal times to plant healthy crops. Many ancient peoples also linked the moon cycle with the menstrual cycle. Because of its associations with fertile soil for crops and the fertility of the womb, the moon has often been connected with creation and the feminine. Worship of the moon has been an accepted part of religions and cultures all across the world. Moon goddesses abound. Many of the moon goddesses are correlated with a face of the triple goddess: maiden, mother, crone. Write your favourite one a thank-you card. Tell her all about your hopes and dreams and share your gratitude at the same time. Give those wishes to the moon.

ARTEMIS (GREEK) DIANA (ROMAN)

Artemis is the Greek personification of the maiden face of the triple moon goddess. Her archetypes are the virgin and the hunter. She wields a silver bow and is a defender of women and children. Her name means "high source of water." She holds the lunar power to control all the oceans, seas, and tides. Work with her energy by meditating on wildness and confidence.

SELENE (GREEK) LUNA (ROMAN)

Selene is the most ancient of the Greek moon goddesses. She personifies the mother face of the triple moon goddess. Her archetype is the lover. Selene bathes the world with her gossamer moonlight kisses. Channel her energy through meditation on themes of sensuality and nurture.

HECATE (GREEK)

The crone face of the triple moon goddess, Hecate's archetype is the sage. Depicted with two torches and a key, she guides people over crossroads and through entryways, and also through the transition from life to death. She holds wisdom of light, divination, magic, intuition, plants, and medicinal herbs. To connect with Hecate, meditate on themes of release and letting go.

CHANG'E, CHANG-E, CH'ANG-O OR CHANG-NGO (CHINESE)

Chang'e is remembered during the mid-autumn or moon festival in China. She is the "woman on the moon" and she lives there accompanied by a jade rabbit. Her archetype is the beautiful one. She embodies quiet Yin energy. Channel Chang'e through meditative reflection and solitude.

MAMA QUILLA (INCA)

Mama Quilla was the Inca goddess of the moon. She was worshipped as the goddess of marriage and the menstrual cycle, and as the defender of women. During an eclipse it was believed that a supernatural jaguar was attacking her. Her tears formed the silver found in the earth. Mama Quilla's archetypes are the mother and the warrior. Work with her energy by meditating on vitality, action, and protection.

RHIANNON (CELTIC)

The name Rhiannon means "night queen." She is a Celtic moon goddess. Her archetypes are the mother and the martyr, and she shares a message of rebirth, wisdom, transformation, and intuition. Call on her to learn patience and forgiveness.

HERBS

Diffuse essential oils, ingest teas (always taking care—check with your herbalist first!) or smudge these herbs to harness and balance the energy of the moon phase.

NEW MOON

Milky oats
Very nutritious; helps you prepare for the work ahead.

Ginger
Awakens.

Lavender
Relaxes. Offers support for the changes ahead.

FULL MOON

Jasmine
Attracts prosperity, rewarding your efforts.

Anise
Balances and harmonizes.

Calendula
Soothes and heals.

FIRST QUARTER

Thyme
Helps you focus and concentrate as you get to work.

Coriander
Harnesses the energy of enthusiasm and spontaneity.

Juniper berry
Offers protection as you increase your level of activity.

THIRD QUARTER

Goldenseal
A cure-all; helps restore cellular health after the active waxing moon phase.

Mugwort
Remedies fatigue.

Eyebright
Gives clear sight moving forward.

CRYSTALS

Crystals have powerful properties to help support your hopes and desires for each moon phase. Use these crystals to manifest your intentions. Place them on your altar or hold them during meditation.

NEW MOON

Labradorite
Helps with intuitive expansion. Use it to tap into the creative power of the new moon.

Rose quartz
Activates the heart chakra, the center of love and emotions. Use this crystal to meditate on the feeling of love. Love is a magnet and will help you attract your desires.

Moonstone
Gives clarity.

FIRST QUARTER

Golden tourmaline
Stimulates confidence and personal power.

Peridot
Promotes increase, prosperity, and well-being.

Pyrite
Aids action and vitality.

FULL MOON

At the full moon, cleanse your crystals in the moonlight.

Jade
Attracts abundance.

Moss agate
Balances and stabilizes—excellent for the high emotions of the full moon.

Stilbite
Brings self-expansion and joy.

THIRD QUARTER

Smoky quartz
Cleanses and grounds.

Jasper
Releases bad habits.

Black tourmaline
Offers protection.

PAUSE AND REFLECT

Congratulations on completing this journey! Take a moment to reflect on your achievements over the course of the year. Let the tidal pull of your connection with the cycles of nature bring you closer to yourself. And get ready to give your brilliant new wishes to the moon, in the next year, and beyond!

Sandy Sitron is an astrologer and consulting hypnotist based in Brooklyn, New York. She has been studying astrology for over twenty years and she received her hypnosis certification from the National Guild of Hypnotists. Sandy combines astrology and hypnosis to help people understand the cycles in their lives and create lasting positive change. She writes for The Numinous and Well+Good and is a wellness practitioner at Maha Rose. Sandy offers private astrology and hypnosis sessions in New York or online. She can be found at www.sandysitron.com.

First published in the United States of America
in 2018 by Chronicle Books LLC.
Originally published in the United Kingdom
in 2017 by Pop Press.

ISBN 978-1-4521-7271-2

Manufactured in China.

Text by Sandy Sitron
Design and illustrations by Therese Vandling

10 9 8 7 6 5

Chronicle books and gifts are available at special quantity
discounts to corporations, professional associations, literacy
programs, and other organizations. For details and discount
information, please contact our premiums department at
corporatesales@chroniclebooks.com or at 1-800-759-0190.

Chronicle Books LLC
680 Second Street
San Francisco, California 94107
www.chroniclebooks.com